LIHE

SENSE AND SENSIBILITY

Some thoughts on the teaching of literacy

Margaret Donaldson

Reading and Language Information Centre
University of Reading   School of Education
London Road, Reading RG1 5AQ

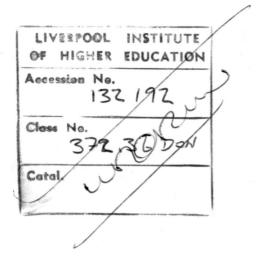
ISBN 0 7049 0895 6

Printed at the College of Estate Management, Reading

CONTENTS

FOREWORD

This paper owes its existence to a discussion I had with Mary Cooper at the annual conference of the United Kingdom Reading Association in 1987. Between then and now she and her colleagues in the Association have encouraged me by their continuing interest in the project. I am particularly indebted to Christine Anderson, who was President of UKRA for the year 1987–88, and to the members of the Publications Committee. Sue Palmer and Peter Brinton of that Committee sent me detailed and thoughtful criticisms that were a great help.

I am also grateful to Alison Elliot, Avril Barton, Peter Gannon, Jane Langley, Lynne Murray, Chris Pratt, Jess Reid and Stephen Salter who took time to read drafts of the paper at various stages and to tell me what they thought of it. Their comments often led me to think again and I have tried to make good use of their advice.

To Jess Reid further special acknowledgement is due. Beyond and behind her specific help in the writing of this paper there lies the history of our many talks over the years on the teaching of literacy. These have been invaluable to me.

25 October 1988   M.D.

4

1 Introduction

The notion has recently gained some currency that reading scarcely needs to be taught at all. No one doubts that it has to be learned and no one doubts, I think, that skilled readers can give learners help. But beyond this point dispute begins. There is deep disagreement in current thinking about the kinds of 'help' that are desirable – the kinds that truly help. And some people have come to believe that what has traditionally been known as 'teaching' is seriously damaging in its effects.

Debates of this kind are apt to become passionate, which is not a bad thing in itself if the passion arises from deeply felt concern and is an outcome of the right kind of caring about the ways in which we educate our children. But we do the children – and the future of our society – no good unless we somehow combine this caring with level-headed reflection on the facts about children and literacy, so far as these are available to us. Sense is needed as well as sensibility.

As to the presentation of the arguments in cases like this where feelings run strong, I agree with Mary Midgeley (1985) that the goal to aim for should be 'the very careful avoidance of all cheap and simple ranting which might carry people away to accept one's views wholesale, but also the full scrupulous expression of attitudes and feelings which seem to one, after thought, to be called for by the subject matter'.

2 The Minimal Teaching Movement

Those who propose radical alternatives to the systematic teaching of literacy do not speak with a single voice. To say this is in no way to make a criticism. Rather it is to recognise that different writers on the subject make different emphases and that any attempt to summarise the general case will fail to do justice to this legitimate diversity. However, I think there is at least one belief that all of them would share: the belief that children are highly active and efficient learners, competent inquirers, eager to understand.

This belief is one that I hold too. I have already argued the case for it (Donaldson, 1978). More and more evidence keeps coming to support the view that it is true of human beings from the earliest months of life. Children's minds are not at any stage – not ever – to be thought of as receptacles into which stuff called knowledge can be poured. Nor do

5

children wait in a general way for us to prod them into learning. They wonder, they question, they try to make sense. And, not infrequently, when they direct their questions at us they push to the limit our ability to answer them, as every adult who has spoken much with children knows.

A striking example of this comes from a boy called Jamie who was three years eleven months old when the following conversation took place.

Jamie and an adult were in a lane beside a house in the country. A car was parked on a concrete base.

Jamie: Why is it on that metal thing?

Adult: It's not metal, it's concrete.

Jamie: Why is it on the concrete thing?

Adult: Well, when it rains the ground gets soft and muddy, doesn't it?

(Jamie nods, bends down and scratches the dry earth.)

Adult: So the wheels would sink into the mud. But the concrete's hard, you see!

Jamie (excitedly):   But the concrete's soft in the mix. Why is it soft in the mix?

The adult, who had not thought of this, found it very hard to explain why earth gets soft and hard and soft again whereas concrete, once set, stays hard forever.

Jamie's father worked in the building trade so Jamie was familiar with concrete mixers. He was a bright little boy but there was nothing to suggest that he was exceptional. Preschool children often show that they think spontaneously in active, searching ways, just as he did, about the world around them.

It follows directly that certain kinds of teaching can be stultifying. This truth is of ancient origin, yet it bears repeating again and again, in case we should forget. Teaching is stultifying whenever it fails to respect the minds of the learners, whenever it discourages the questioning, whenever it frustrates the desire to understand.

Disgust with teaching which has failed seriously in these ways often rises strongly in sensitive people. They are then tempted to take a further step, leading on to the conclusion that the less we teach the better. After all, if children are so good at learning, why not let them get on with it? Shouldn't we just be content to provide material facilities and such encouragement as seems appropriate from time to time? Shouldn't we in fact stop being teachers and become consultants?

These arguments are attractive, seductive even. But the step of answering 'yes' to them should be recognised for the very large and risky one that it is. Some teaching is damaging; but this certainly does not lead with any necessity to the conclusion that all teaching is damaging and that we can very well do without it. Also the fact that children are active, competent learners does not imply that there is no place for active, competent teaching.

Later I shall be making a positive case for such teaching in the specific field of literacy. First, however, I want to consider how the idea that teaching should be minimal is currently being applied in that same context.

This application generally takes the form of a proposal that we should give the children 'real books' and encourage them to 'learn to read by reading'. It takes also the more negative form of a generalised rejection of anything that can be called a 'reading scheme'. Indeed, in practice the term 'real books' is often quite negatively defined: a 'real book' seems to be one that does not form part of any set of books systematically planned with the primary aim of helping children to learn to read.

I say advisedly that the term has come to be so defined *in practice.* Of course some thoughtful writers on the subject have given more positive criteria. Margaret Meek, for instance, requires that '. . . the pictures help the reader to understand the story, that the story has a shape and the author a voice'. (Meek, 1982, p 66). She does not offer this as an explicit definition, but from the way she uses the term 'real books' further down the page we may reasonably conclude that she has been saying what she understands a 'real book' to be.

Meek's criteria are good ones by which to judge the quality of fiction for young children, whether that fiction forms part of a planned

7

programme or not. The mistake is to replace careful consideration of quality by a general condemnation of reading schemes.

This mistake is serious, and when one stops to think, it is very strange. I recently told an educator from overseas that in parts of this country books were now being judged unacceptable for no other reason than that they were published as 'schemes', and he refused to believe me.

When 'real books' are placed in absolute contrast to all reading schemes, the implications are very far-reaching. What is then being said is that books written for the purpose of helping children to learn to read cannot help them. We are not being told that some – or even all – of the books that have been written for this purpose up to now have failed to achieve it. We are being told that all such books are necessarily bad because of this property of being 'not real'. The implication is that the entire attempt should be abandoned.

It is essential to recognise that the older traditional reading schemes had grave faults, some of which are perpetuated in the less enlightened modern ones. I shall have more to say later about the nature of these faults and the reasons for them (see pages 19–20). Briefly, these reasons lay in a poor understanding of how children think and learn. But I believe we have made good progress in this regard over recent decades; and to use the old failures as a basis for rejection is like using pre-Newtonian conceptions of the natural world as a reason for no longer trying to apply physics (1).

If we decide that children are to be offered nothing systematically devised to help them, then the gates are closed against the use of any detailed knowledge that we may have, or might obtain, about the processes by which children do in fact become literate. We are not to concern ourselves with how this is done – not at least with the aim of applying anything that we already know or might ever come to know about, say, specific difficulties that children are likely to encounter when tackling certain kinds of text. The systematic help that might derive from such knowledge is deliberately to be withheld.

Put like this, it is a curious conclusion, but I do not think I state it too strongly. The rejection of *all* published reading programmes, however good the insights on which they are based, however enlightened their guiding principles, however good the stories they contain, has just this implication.

Those who urge such a blanket rejection have certainly no desire to refuse children help. I do not doubt the sincerity of their conviction that 'real books – no schemes' will provide the best help possible. So how are we to make sense of their position? Another widely held belief is crucial to the understanding of it. This is the belief that the learning of written language is essentially the same kind of thing as the learning of spoken language.

Children, as we all know, learn to speak and to understand speech without depending on systematic instruction. They start to do this spontaneously within the first eighteen months of life, given that they are spoken to in ordinary, natural ways (which as a rule are not consciously planned). In these circumstances most children 'latch on' readily, and soon learn to make sense of the speech that is all around them (2). So then, the argument goes, the same holds for written language. Away with schemes!

These views are made quite explicit in a paper by Goodman (1972). The paper is full of optimism about the future. It begins with the sentence:

'It is entirely possible that within the next decade virtually all children will be learning to read, easily and effectively.'

All we can say, looking back, is that it may have been possible but it has certainly not happened.

Goodman thought that this achievement would follow not from better teaching but from less teaching. Universal literacy would come easily if only teachers would 'stop interfering with learners in the name of helping them'. And learners would be able to manage the task because 'reading is a language process, the direct counterpart of listening'.

Goodman offers some effective criticism of the older kinds of reading instruction that were based on inappropriate theories. He also makes some important positive emphases. But his enthusiasm for the new insights into children's power and creativity as first language learners (insights stemming from the work of Chomsky) leads him to conclusions that are seriously flawed.

The main weakness of Goodman's case lies in an over-emphasis on the similarities between speech and writing. It is true that both are 'language processes' but they are in many ways different, as Vygotsky (1962) saw clearly (3). To my mind the notion that the differences can be ignored in educational practice is profoundly mistaken and dangerous. Much of my later argument will be concerned to explain why.

First, however, we have still to consider a further, related claim that is made by some advocates of minimal teaching in the field of literacy. It is this: *As one reads one need not attend to the words on the page.*

At this point we must go very carefully or we shall run into confusion. The sentence in italics is ambiguous. It could be taken to mean that the act of reading is not dependent on attention to individual words – that it is possible to 'get the meaning' directly, without having to be aware of the words that are its vehicle. On the other hand, the sentence could mean that attending to the words on the page is not an important thing ever to do – that it does not ever make our reading better.

On the first interpretation the sentence makes a claim (rightly or wrongly) as to fact. On the second interpretation it expresses a judgment about the value of reading in one particular way. If we confuse a factual claim with a value judgment we are in serious intellectual difficulty; yet it is all too easy to slide from one to the other without noticing what we are doing. And what can save us from this kind of sliding and slithering? Only close, thoughtful attention to the words on the page.

In the first – the factual – sense, the claim that we need not attend to individual words is well founded as it applies to skilled readers (though I very much doubt its truth when applied to beginners). Once we are sufficiently sophisticated and aware of ourselves as readers it is an option we have. We can read with more or less close attention to the words on the page before us. We can move along, when we judge this to be appropriate, making some kind of rapid sense. Or we can pause for thought, ask questions as to meanings, try to detect muddle and to avoid potential misunderstanding.

Interpreted in the second possible way, the sentence in italics would mean that the latter kind of reading is unimportant, something that we *need not* bother to cultivate, either in ourselves or in those we teach. It would mean that we should not place a high value on the ability to read reflectively, thinking about the words and their meanings, noticing how they function, how they interact; for it is impossible to give text close reflective scrutiny without attending to the words on the page. Notice that the devaluing of attention to words devalues poetry just as much as it endangers clarity of thought (4).

Frank Smith (1978) tells us that reading without noticing the words is 'normal' (5). This view is closely related to the notion that learning written language is much the same kind of process as learning spoken language. When children learn to interpret speech they do not for the most part consciously attend to the words they hear. This is well established. They do not concern themselves with word meanings, but rather with a perception of the total meaning of utterances in context. We may say that for young children, an utterance is *embedded* in its context, is never considered apart from its context (6). And this embedding context includes, most importantly, what is seen as the purpose of the speaker. It is no exaggeration to say that children are concerned most of the time with what people mean, not with what words mean. Yet somehow – and this is a large part of what makes first language learning so remarkable and so intriguing – they learn enough about words at some level of consciousness to be able to put them together and express new meanings of their own.

So this is what children actually do as they learn spoken language. And at first they could do no other. It is the way human beings learn to speak. It does not follow that they can effectively learn to read in the same way.

I must now explain why I am convinced that literacy learning differs profoundly from the learning of the mother tongue.

3   The Learning of Spoken and Written Language

The name *mother tongue* is entirely appropriate, for language learning arises out of the earliest mutual enterprises of child and mother (or other adult in the mother's place). It arises spontaneously as interesting things occur that call for comment or action. It arises in connection with purposes, shared or conflicting; with social games; with the solving of problems where help is needed. It is combined with gesture in ways that McNeill (1987) has shown to be of fundamental importance. It has the most intimate connection with emotion – with laughter and tears, with teasing and comfort, with pleasure and anger. It is intensely immediate and personal.

In these early experiences mental life has a unified, a seamless, quality. 'Thoughts', 'language' and 'feelings' are integrally bound up with one another. And with them, too, are interwoven perception and purposive action. Young children talk at first about what they can see happening here and now, and what they are doing and feeling about it. There are extensions beyond the present into the very recent past and the very near future, extensions involving some consideration of what has just happened or what is just about to happen. But these reach at first only far enough to guarantee continuously evolving experience.

Gradually, of course, the range widens and children start to talk about things more remote in space and time. However, there is usually little of this until the third year of life is on its way, by which time a considerable linguistic competence has been established (7).

Consider now what these facts imply for the claim that written language is learned in the same way as spoken language. If this claim were sound, then written language would also have to arise spontaneously in the course of other shared activities, with all the give and take and immediacy of speech. Reading and writing – both of them – would have to be used by adult *and by child* to communicate about ongoing events, to ask for or offer help, to question and to answer, to reproach, to amuse. They would have to be used for the spontaneous expression of human feelings – surprise, wonder, love, hate, relief, fear.

It is quite evident that they are not used in this way. But now a question at once arises: why not? Is there any intrinsic difference between spoken and written language that prevents it? A space travel fantasy may help to make the answer plain.

Let us imagine a planet inhabited by beings called Browfolk. The Browfolk are just like ourselves except that they have little windows set into their foreheads in which graphic symbols can appear, coming into view at one end and moving across to disappear at the other. Forehead symbols accompany most of the social activities of these beings, contributing greatly to the success of their co-operative endeavours. Also the symbols may appear in different colours, expressive of states of feeling. When one of the Browfolk is angry, the forehead symbols show up in fiery red. A soft blue expresses tender affection, a greyish brown expresses boredom and so on.

Sometimes a shutter closes over the window. But we are informed by returning space explorers that, behind the shutter, symbols are still regularly being produced for the private purposes of the individual concerned. Explorers also report that Browfolk children learn to produce and interpret the forehead symbols with precisely the same speed and ease as human children learn to manage the sounds of the mother tongue. They learn these symbols in the course of communicating about things that matter to them, things significant to them because of what they are seeing, feeling and doing at the time. Written symbols are, so to speak, their mother brow.

Human beings, however, do not have a mother brow. We do not use written symbols for the spontaneous expression of thoughts and emotions in our direct 'face-to-face' dealings with one another. So for us the learning of these symbols – how to produce them, how to make sense of them – is a profoundly different enterprise from the learning of speech. It is so because of our biological nature.

4 Links between Spoken and Written Language

And yet we are odd creatures. Paradoxically, we have the kind of biology that sometimes lets us transcend our biology. We fly without wings, after all. So, in spite of the deep difference between spoken and written language, it is worth asking how close human literacy learning can come to the embedded learning of speech.

As Reid (1983) has pointed out, there are at least four means by which bridges, or links, can be established.

a *Shared reading*
First, an adult and a child can look at a book together. To begin with, when the child is quite young, this is often mainly a way by which the

range of knowledge of *spoken* language is extended. Some parents use books quite deliberately for this purpose. Olson (1984) suggests that such parents (who tend of course to be highly literate themselves) are actually teaching oral language 'somewhat systematically' to their children, drawing attention to the names of things and even sometimes to verbs or other parts of speech. He argues that in so doing these parents are using analytic methods taken over from the practice of teaching reading, and that they are encouraging the notion of language as something to talk about and think about, not merely to use unreflectingly. They are thus laying oral foundations for literacy. It is an important idea, to which I shall return later. But obviously early books are – and should be – used in other ways.

As children grow older they can move, within the same book-sharing context, from oral language learning to the start of reading. And to begin in this way brings advantages that have lately often been noted. These can be very significant. If all is well, the child will be sitting close to an adult with whom there is a warm, comforting, supportive relationship. This will be a pleasurable experience, there will be emotion in it. Also, as the adult reads aloud, the intonation of the voice will be used to express suspense, surprise, humour or whatever, as the story requires. This is good and helpful as a means of first encounter with those static marks on the page that must later be dealt with on their own. And it is a good informal introduction to story-telling language.

But of course not every child experiences reading shared with a friendly adult, or is likely to do so in any human culture close at hand. Further we must recognise that the advantages are diminished or can even turn into drawbacks when children are unwilling or adults unwise. Dunn (1987) found from her observation of two-year-olds that reading was often 'resorted to' by mothers when children were tired or fractious and that it was not usually 'an idyllic moment of rapport'. Similar findings are reported by Tizard and Hughes (1984) from work with four-year-olds.

The teaching of reading solely through the use of 'real books' has to involve some kind of sharing, even though the techniques of shared reading do not depend on the use of 'real books'. Thus the 'real books' movement relies on the hope that children can be given good experiences of shared reading on a regular basis in school (and of course ideally at home too). But real books have to be used by real teachers in real classrooms, where the class is likely to contain around thirty very real children. In these circumstances sustained one-to-one contact will often be hard to achieve.

So practical difficulties alone can make shared reading unsuitable as the sole way of helping beginners to learn. I do not, however, believe that it has no place in school. My thesis is that help towards literacy has to come from many sources, among which shared reading has its place. There will be times when one child can have the teacher's undivided attention. At other times the sharing can be not with a single child but with a small group, provided that multiple copies of the book can be obtained. Chosen stories can be made available on tape, so that a child can listen alone to the sound of familiar words while following the text. The help of adult volunteers or competent older children can be enlisted, and they can be given guidance on how best to handle the book-sharing. These activities now form a recognised part of the teaching of literacy in many schools.

b   *Helping children to produce written language*

The next way of bringing literacy learning closer to that of speech is the one most obviously concerned with transcending biological limitations. A big difference between speech and writing is that young children cannot produce written language easily, whereas they are well equipped with the ability to produce speech sounds. There is great merit, therefore, in the provision of a set of printed words for children to use in the construction of their own sentences.

Notice, however, that the use of words on cards to construct sentences is altogether different from the use of 'flash cards'. The practice of making children learn to read isolated words out of context dates back to old discredited associationist theories of reading and it is not a good idea. It is not a good idea because it neglects the importance of making sense. However, when children put word cards together to form sentences, making sense is precisely the aim. At the same time their awareness of language is raised in many valuable ways. They are helped to notice such features as word boundaries, word order, bound morphemes (-s, -ed, -ing, etc.) but all in the course of the expression of meaning (see the evaluation of 'Breakthrough to Literacy' by Reid, 1974).

c   Use of print embedded in the environment

As we move on now to the third way of linking oral and written language, it will be helpful to notice that there are two distinct senses in which a word may be presented to a child in or out of 'context'. There is the sense of linguistic context which we have just been considering. However, there also exist non-linguistic contexts for language. We saw earlier the role that these play in speech, and we took stock of the fact that language on the page of a book has to manage without them (aside from the help given by illustrations). Yet there is one special circumstance in which written words, like spoken words, enjoy the support of a non-linguistic context. I refer to a form of writing that is all around us – above shop windows, inside supermarkets, on buses and bus-stops, on medicine bottles – and is often called public or ambient print. This has the merit that children see it everywhere. But it has the deeper merit of being closely related to the non-linguistic context in which it occurs. To put 'sugar' above the bags of salt or 'fire escape' above the door that leads to the linen cupboard is to invite comical or dangerous results. Assuming, however, that such errors are avoided, the setting supports understanding. Children can easily grasp the communicative purpose of printed signs, and the context helps them to get the meaning. In this respect public print – which I prefer to call 'embedded' print – is like the speech that children learn when language learning begins.

Intelligent use can be made of this fact in helping children at the very first steps of literacy learning. Many opportunities for using embedded print present themselves in the classroom where, for instance, labels and notices can be displayed. But the labels should be functional – they should serve a real communicative purpose that the children can recognise. It is good to put 'pencils' on a drawer or box containing pencils which are out of sight. It is not so good to attach a label to a chair saying 'chair'. To learn about embedded print is to learn that written language is a way in which people convey meaning to one another. This can be of particular help when one is working with children whose preschool experience of books is limited.

An interesting question now arises: if embedded print can be useful in school, could it also be used successfully with much younger children in the home? Could a child who is learning to speak – a child of two, say – be introduced to written language in an embedded form and start to learn to interpret it in parallel with speech? And would this stimulate later development towards full literacy?

A number of people who have tried this believe that it works. The method was proposed by Doman (1964) and greeted with scorn by most professional educators and academic psychologists. However, Ragnhild Söderbergh, a Swedish psycholinguist, having tried it on her own daughter and reviewed a number of other studies, is far from dismissive. She believes that a very young child may discover that written words correspond to spoken words and, like them, convey meaning. But for this to be possible '. . . a very close interaction with reading and writing people is necessary, an interaction that is meaningful to the child and where writing is adapted to the child's general cognitive and linguistic development'. (Söderbergh, 1981, p 207.)

At first children who start to learn in this way tend to treat the written words as if they were the things they stand for. Thus Söderbergh's daughter, at age two-and-a-half, pushed the card for 'pram' around the floor. And another child put the card for 'Daddy' on top of the card bearing the name of a horse and said: 'Now Daddy is sitting on Dusty'.

Also at first – and not surprisingly – children seem to treat the words as ideographs. However, they gradually learn the alphabetic principle and become interested in grapheme-phoneme correspondences. That is, they start to inquire about phonics.

Söderbergh tells us that it is important to begin with the names of things that are very significant for the child: the child's own name, of course, and the names of pets, favourite toys or objects of special interest. Verbs and adjectives can follow; and 'emotionally coloured' words like *happy, sad* or *cry* tend to be easily learned. As with nouns, the word may scarcely be regarded as separate from what it means. Thus 'frightful' is considered frightening. This points to the profoundly embedded nature of the experience.

Söderbergh claims that, from this kind of beginning, very good later progress follows. But success clearly depends on the presence of a literate adult with a good understanding of the right guiding principles, with much patience and sensitivity and with lots of time to spare.

d   Use of the patterns of children's speech

The fourth way of narrowing the gap between written and spoken language is in some respects the most important of all. To appreciate its significance one must first recognise that, although writing is a means by which spoken words may be rendered visible and permanent, written language is not just 'speech written down'. Indeed, when speech *is* written down verbatim – as, for instance, when conference proceedings are transcribed from a tape recording – the resulting text makes very curious reading indeed.

The fact is that written language differs structurally from speech in a multitude of ways. There are many things which we write but would not be at all likely to say, at least in everyday informal talk. Consider, for example:

The prince, for that is who he was, took her hand.

Sue was not a girl to give up readily.

The ogre's eyes fell upon the floor.

Not all the Indians stayed upon the shore.

Second only to man, the great apes are the most intelligent of all animals.

Not one of these sentence forms would be regularly produced in the course of ordinary spontaneous conversation with children, or indeed in the speech of most adults to one another.

There exists, in effect, a rich and complex 'language of books'. Skilled adult readers are so used to it that they hardly notice the divergences from the spoken tongue, but it presents formidable problems for beginners because it confounds their expectations and frustrates their attempts at intelligent prediction. This is particularly true of children who do not come from highly literate homes; but the confusion and frustration are by no means confined to this group, large as it is. Novice readers from all kinds of background can be heard to stumble and falter – and often to groan in despair – when the text they are asked to read is not written in the kind of language they know, and consequently does not make sense to them (8).

We know from many studies over the last thirty years that children bring their expectations to bear on their reading even in the very early stages (see, for instance, Clay, 1969; Weber, 1970). They try to structure and predict in highly reasonable ways, for they are reasonable beings who already know a great deal about spoken language and about the world around them. It is interesting, however, that when problems of mistaken prediction arise ('miscues' in Goodman's terminology), the children themselves are generally not conscious of the nature of the difficulties they are experiencing although they know very well that they are in trouble. Reid (1958) asked children of five to read aloud a number of sentences of which the following are examples:

i   I can see his face in the darkness.

ii   We went back to the deep mud.

iii Darkness was upon the face of the deep.

Sentences (i) and (ii) were fairly easy, but (iii) was very difficult. The children's own explanation was that (iii) contained 'hard words' which they had not seen before – namely 'darkness', 'face' and 'deep'. They seemed to be unaware of having read the same words successfully a few seconds earlier. It is worth noting that the children in this study were attending a fee-paying school where the general standards of literacy were high.

The idea that 'hard words' are the sole source of reading difficulty is an old one, and not by any means confined to children. It used to be very widely believed that if you can read a word you can read it anywhere. In other words, linguistic context was ignored. Language structures were not thought of as important. We know better now – and Reid's study was a pioneering one on the way to our new knowledge. But we do not always apply this knowledge as well as we might. For example, as I mentioned earlier, children are still often asked to learn isolated words on cards, a practice to be deplored.

It used also to be believed that short, phonically 'regular' words were necessarily the easiest kind. One early reading scheme was based on this conviction with tragic/comic results. The first book was restricted to words containing no more than two letters.

You may ask: Is this possible? Never underestimate human ingenuity. Here are some examples:

I am on an ox. Is he on an ox? An ox is by me.

Other, less determined, writers of the early 'primers' settled for three-letter words, and we got cats on mats and sentences like 'See, see!' or 'Run, Bob, run!'.

Reading programmes that depended on these mistaken notions were, as I said earlier, very bad. They cannot be defended, except on the grounds that the truth was not obvious till the right kind of research had been done (9).

The gross demerits of texts based on 'short easy word' theories have had much to do with the development of the stereotype of the 'reading scheme' and thus with the blanket rejection of all books written with the aim of making the beginner's task easier. But it is a very far cry from the early primers to books based on an understanding of the last of the four ways of narrowing the gap between learning to read and learning to speak. This fourth way, as will by now be evident, consists in providing text that comes close to the structural patterns of the children's speech.

I say 'comes close' because we are not, even here, dealing with speech written down. Children's actual speech, directly transcribed, would, like conference proceedings, contain features making it quite inappropriate for the printed page. There would be incomplete sentences, unexplained references to context, a lack of continuity and so on. Nor are we talking about text which contains a high proportion of conversation, even if this were edited to avoid the incoherence of actual speech. For it turns out that dialogue is at first hard to read.

The kind of text we need can be quite varied and flexible as to content, but the essential thing is that it should be based on knowledge of the kinds of grammatical structure which children commonly use and which they will therefore expect to find.

Text of this kind will give beginners the best chance of predicting intelligently, for it will enable them to use their pre-existing linguistic knowledge to the full. It will avoid, initially, those ways of expression that belong to 'the language of books' – ways which do not just use harder vocabulary but which turn sentences differently, use more complex ways of connecting ideas, shorten by deletion and obey a whole set of linguistic conventions that have to be learned. Some examples were given on page 18.

20

Books that are free from such features yet avoid mistaken and stultifying notions of simplicity can give great support to early sense-making efforts. And as Meek (1985) says: 'The most important thing is the learner's belief that he can turn print into sense' (10). Speaking of children who were reading the first few books in a modern programme of this kind, a wise and experienced teacher once said to me: 'It's amazing! The words just come tripping off their tongues'.

The first books in such a programme may not contain 'stories'. But they can contain language that is true to genuine and important uses of print – ways of captioning pictures, describing scenes and narrating events which do not violate accepted usage yet which stay within the grammatical constraints of children's speech. They will serve purposes that are different from the purposes of shared stories, but that complement them. If their content is relatively familiar then the children's minds are not pre-occupied with imaginative reconstruction (which is more demanding than is often recognised) and so are free to focus on sense-making of a simpler kind.

Once children have acquired some basic skill and ease at this level, the text can gradually incorporate features of book language which will enrich its resources and widen its scope.

Make no mistake, however – such books look simple but this does not make them easy to write. To be effective, they must be informed by a very good knowledge of language development. Margaret Meek likes to describe the best children's literature as 'crafted'. She is right, it is a good term. But a book of the kind we have been considering will have to be crafted too, in its own kind of way, if it is to be any good at all.

One piece of research which gave a major impetus to the study of reading book text and its relation to children's speech was a monograph by Strickland (1962). In her conclusions, Strickland emphasised the poverty and stiltedness of the old-fashioned texts by comparison with the variety found in her recordings of childrens speech – a variety stemming in part from ways of combining statements by the use of connectives, especially 'and', 'but' and 'so'. The traditional use of short one-clause sentences in reading schemes often resulted in very poor cohesion, rhythm and flow. The improvement when these simple connectives are used can be very marked. But they have to be handled with discretion.

A subsequent study by Reid (1970), using some of Strickland's speech data, analysed four reading schemes which were then in common use in Britain. Focussing on the other aspect of the comparison Reid looked for structures that were common in the texts but absent from the speech samples. For example, the text might contain sentences beginning in ways that young children never use, such as: 'In the box he found . . .'. A further example concerns the handling of dialogue. As I mentioned earlier, dialogue in stories is difficult for early learners to read. First words in quoted utterances may be hard to predict. Questions may not be spotted for what they are. The switching of 'voices' can be confusing to follow. Matters are made worse when quoted speech comes before any information about who is speaking, and worse still if that information is given in the literary inverted form ('said so-and-so'). These structures do not occur in speech samples from children so they have to be learned from the printed page or from hearing stories read aloud.

One form of presentation of dialogue with a long tradition in comics and cartoons is the 'speech bubble'. This convention links the quoted words to the appropriate character in the illustration and can thus provide helpful support, especially if the quoted words are repeated in the text. What is very bad, on the other hand, is for the text to consist entirely of 'pseudo-dialogue'. This was a form much used in traditional primers, and was one of the features that laid them open to ridicule and parody (the 'Look, look, look' style of text). The same kind of thing occurs, unfortunately, in texts still in use today. One may find, scattered about on the page, words such as 'Help' which are clearly meant to be spoken by a character shown in the illustration but which are not attributed to that character in any way. The learner must therefore identify the words *before* trying to infer who uttered them. Surely this is to stand prediction on its head.

* * * * * *

To summarise, then, the four gap-narrowers we have considered are: shared reading; devices which make it possible to produce sentences without forming letters by hand; embedded print; and the provision of books in which the language is based on the structures of children's own speech. These bridges, if they are used intelligently and sensitively, make good starting-points on the way to becoming literate. Each has its own distinctive contribution, each can help. All four together can help greatly. But they are only starting-points. What is to follow is a whole new kind of enterprise.

5   Literacy: The New Enterprise

So far we have been thinking about the beginning of literacy and how this relates to what went before. We have been looking backwards to the competences that children bring to the learning task. We have been considering what is new in it for them, what is hard about it, how they can be helped to get begun.

I want now to change direction and emphasis. This will mean looking quite far ahead, while at the same time shifting the focus from problems to the long-term opportunities that literacy affords. These are evidently many; but I shall concentrate here on one kind – the kind that I think is most in danger of being obscured by current ideas about minimal teaching.

We have seen that language written down is thereby cut loose – or disembedded – from the context of ongoing activities and feelings in which speech functions and on which speech thrives. *Once on the page, language is on its own.* This gives it a degree of independence which makes it particularly apt for the development and the expression of certain kinds of thought. I have in mind thought that is about general topics with no immediate bearing on the personal life. For instance, how do birds find their way when they migrate? Or why does concrete set hard?

Human beings have in them an urge to understand. This urge carries them beyond their own immediate personal concerns towards the search for *general* understanding. It takes them in the direction of the search for truth.

The desire to understand, even in cases where understanding seems unlikely to bring any practical personal gain, certainly comes before literacy both in the history of the human species and in the history of individuals. Jamie was not literate when he eagerly wanted to know why concrete, unlike mud, is soft in the mix then stays hard forever (see page 6). But though the search for understanding does not come from literacy, literacy can greatly advance and further it. It does this in at least two ways.

The first and very obvious way is that it enables us to learn from other people whom we cannot personally know. Jamie tried to get understanding from a person who was with him but who could not help.

If he had been fully literate he could have taken his question to a whole range of people otherwise inaccessible – those who have written books on 'materials science' or civil engineering. As it was, he was frustrated.

The second effect is on thinking itself – especially on the ability to sustain thought and to put thought in order. Jamie's command of spoken language enabled him to engage in a very interesting brief sequence of intelligent reflection. However, humanity has developed great *systems* of thought; and literacy is essential for anyone who is going to take any part, however modest, in the systematic enterprise.

Engaging in this enterprise means trying to think clearly and rigorously and to hold to trains of argument. It means asking oneself questions about one's own thinking. Is there vagueness in it, or self-contradiction? Does it make the important distinctions? Is anything left out that should have been considered? In this attempt it is of the greatest help to be able to write one's thoughts down. It then becomes much easier to criticise them and re-order them in the effort after clarity and power.

What I am saying is that *the thinking itself draws great strength from literacy* whenever it is more than just a scrap of an idea, whenever there is a discussion to develop, whenever there are complex possibilities to consider. It is even more obvious that the sustained, orderly *communication* of this kind of thinking requires a considerable mastery of the written word.

a   *The language of systematic thought*

Let us now take an example of a topic that calls for thought going beyond personal experience. Consider the question of violence in modern society: is it increasing and, if so, why? Someone who is writing about this may well have relevant first-hand knowledge. The topic may bear on her own life. There may have been some incidence of violence in her family. But what she must write – if she is to tackle the general question adequately – is not merely an account of these events. She must not just describe how Auntie Flo was mugged. She may use some of the knowledge thus gained, but she must reach beyond any personal involvement to general issues. She has first to question whether violence is indeed on the increase. If she decides it is, she must entertain hypotheses about causes. And so on.

In this sense, the thinking is impersonal. I do not mean that it is not about people or about things that matter to people. The example just given should make this clear. But it is not restricted to the thinker's own life-experiences. It goes beyond these in search of more general understanding.

There is at the moment a powerful movement in our schools the aim of which is to encourage children to write about their own experiences from a very personal point of view. It is good that they should do this. It is *not* good that they should do it exclusively. If all the prose they learn to write is narrative or descriptive then they are being deprived. They need to learn gradually, over the school years, how to participate in the impersonal modes of thinking and of linguistic expression that are such an important part of our cultural heritage.

We have seen that, compared with speech, *all* language on the page has a quality of detachment from the personal life. But the kind of written language we are now concerned with is also *more impersonal in the details of its form*. It entails the use of phrases like: 'It is possible that . . .' or 'The causes of this seem to lie . . .' or 'One reason is . . .' or 'What this means is . . .'.

The degree of this impersonality is to some extent a matter of style and it can be overdone. I reject (as my own writing – even this sentence – shows) the exaggeration which holds it improper to say 'I' or 'in my opinion' when writing on an impersonal theme. Nevertheless a repertoire of impersonal turns of phrase like the examples just given is a great help in the writing of such prose and indispensable for the reading of most of it. Language like this is a sub-class of the language of books. We may call it the language of systematic thought.

Those who cannot handle the language of systematic thought are at a gross disadvantage in every field of study from gardening to astronomy. Some striking examples are to be found in one of the new core texts for GCSE history, *Conflict in Ireland* (McAleavy, 1987), prepared as part of the 'History 13–16' project by the School Curriculum Development Committee. Here, in a way that accords with current thinking on history teaching, original source material is used alongside the author's text. Having been written originally for adults, this material makes no concessions to unsophisticated readers, as the following extracts will show.

'No one who has not been in Ireland during the past six weeks can possibly realise how passionate is the resentment which has been aroused by conscription' (p 67).

'Since such benefits were not available in the south, the idea of a united Ireland as the only way to make things better began to weaken' (p 75).

But even aside from such quotations the main text of the course calls for considerable reading maturity. In the following example, things that people demanded and thought are represented in impersonal, abstract terms:

'The call for a more "Irish Ireland" led to the development of new political ideas. These questioned the need for any sort of link between Ireland and Britain' (p 64).

The reader has to be able to understand that 'The call . . .' is another way of saying 'When people demanded . . .'; that '. . . led to . . . ideas' means 'people began to think differently about politics'; and that while 'These' in the second sentence refers grammatically to 'ideas' the questioning was in the minds of the political thinkers.

Again, here are two of the questions which pupils have to consider:

How did these causes lead to the triumph of Sinn Fein? (p 64)

What impact has Ireland's conflict had on the wider world? (p 86)

Once more the language is highly impersonal.

In many subjects that are studied in secondary school there are also special language problems connected with the precise definition of terms. Often these terms are ordinary words that have been given a particular meaning, like *wave,* or *work,* or *power.* Pupils studying physics have to detach the word 'wave' from everyday notions of (say) the seaside, and the word 'work' from all associations with 'a job'. The precise definition has to be attended to and learned, not just by rote but within the limits of its scientific context. In mathematics the notion of *raising a number to a power* must similarly be detached from everyday expressions like 'the power of the law'.

Is it then reasonable to suppose that the majority of children will be able just to 'pick up' the language of systematic thought, especially if their reading experience consists mainly of stories? I think not. The argument for giving well planned help with the learning of this kind of language throughout the later primary years and into the secondary school seems to me to be very strong.

A good example of sense and balance in regard to the teaching of English is to be found in the revised arrangements for the Scottish Standard Grade examinations (1987) (the equivalent of GCSE) where it is recognised that:

'Language skills do not simply mature in the fullness of time; their development requires conscious cultivation' (p 4).

The document argues for explicit teaching of the main ways in which 'sentences are constructed and punctuated', 'devices of structure and style are used', 'spoken language differs from written forms', 'language is manipulated for different purposes'. Yet the aims are in no way narrow. To quote from the document again: '. . . they (the pupils) need experiences of language which will extend them intellectually, imaginatively, morally, emotionally'. I can only agree.

b   *Laying the foundations of literacy*

Now teachers of young children may feel inclined to say that all this has nothing to do with them – that the problems involved arise later and can be dealt with later. I can understand this attitude but I think it is mistaken, for it underestimates the importance of what happens in the early years. It does not sufficiently recognise the significance of *the way in which children are first taught to read,* and in particular whether this is such as to encourage them to be thoughtful about language right from the start and to look on it as a flexible system over which they can gradually extend their power. The ability to deal with sophisticated impersonal prose of the kind we have been considering does not leap up suddenly when needed like the genie from Aladdin's lamp. It is the outcome of years of sustained direction towards an ultimate goal. If primary teachers do not recognise this they are failing to see the scope and reach of their own importance.

Written language has been used for many purposes in different cultures since it was first invented. For instance, Shirley Brice Heath

(1986) cites the Tuaregs of the Sahara as using it only for graffiti on desert rocks, for talismans and for brief love notes. She also makes the point that, within a given sub-culture in a modern western society, the generally accepted uses of literacy may not include those usually emphasised in school; and further that good initial teaching of children should not fail to take account of their community norms. This is true. We must recognise, therefore, that 'literacy' can quite properly be defined in a variety of ways. However for the purposes of the present discussion I think it is hard to improve on the definition proposed by Olson (1984).

Olson defines literate people as those for whom 'language is known as language'. Literate people are aware of language as an artefact – a structure composed of words and sentences which, as Olson puts it, is 'somewhat independent of the meaning intended by the speaker.' Such people are used to regarding language as an object that one can talk about, study, analyse.

In a metaphor which has become deservedly famous, Courtney Cazden (1974) spoke of language as being either transparent or opaque. When it is transparent, as it typically is in ordinary use, we see meanings *through* it. But when we learn to make it opaque we can look *at* it and think *about* it. This is close to what Olson is saying. Literate people know how to make language opaque when it suits their purpose to do so. And they tend to encourage their children to do this while the children are still learning to speak, before reading has begun. That is, they talk to their children about words, not just with words, helping them to notice what is being said and what they themselves are saying. Olson argues – and I agree with him – that this kind of background experience stands children in very good stead when they make their first serious attempts to deal with the written word, for they already have some of the attitudes to language which are most appropriate and helpful.

It follows, of course, that such children are at a great advantage – as we know them to be in practice – by comparison with those from homes where literacy, in Olson's sense, is lacking. And the latter tend to be the least privileged among us in other respects as well. However, all children can benefit from positive help in learning to handle written language in ways fitting to its nature and to its scope as an instrument of thought. This help must be given bit by bit and with sensitivity in the early stages; but I believe that, with this proviso, the sooner it is begun the better. The teacher of reading can start quite early to encourage conscious, reflective ways of considering the written word. This may not be essential at first, though it can be very helpful even then, but it unobtrusively lays the foundations for much that is to follow.

Once the earliest stages are over and children are at ease with text that is fairly simply structured and does not present too many perplexities of wording, there comes a long period, extending through the primary years, when they must gain increasing mastery, as readers, of the language of books, including the language of systematic thought. They need now to enlarge their understanding of the many ways in which words can be handled with skill on the printed page – handled to achieve economy, or elegance, or emphasis, or surprise, or cohesion between sentences, or logical clarity in a sustained argument, to name only a few of the aims that may concern an author.

In learning about the meanings which these novel ways of wording carry, and about the power they bring, children will also begin to make them their own – part of their repertoire as writers. And the chances of their doing this effectively will be greatly increased if they can develop the ability, as they read, to switch at will to a close examination of unfamiliar or puzzling sequences, while at the same time making their best hypothesis about what the meaning might be.

In trying to lay the foundations of literacy we should never underestimate the difficulty of the task we set children in the secondary schools. We require of them a kind of thinking that does not come spontaneously to the human mind. The urge towards it is there, but the possibility of its mature development depends on a long cultural heritage; and of this heritage the special literate ways of handling language form an essential part. Primary teachers have a crucial role to play in ensuring that the bases of this kind of competence with the written word are well established when a child crosses the secondary school threshold for the first time. If it is not done by then, it will very likely to be too late.

c   *Literacy and social power*

The arguments in this section so far may seem to lack balance – and, indeed, as I have managed to state them so far, they do lack balance. But one cannot say everything at once. I used to have a teacher who, without reading further, seized on the first sentence of every essay and criticised it at great length for what it did not contain! I must now try to correct what would otherwise end up as a poor representation of my own views.

I do not hold that preparation for later schooling should be the only goal of the early school years. These have their own intrinsic claims, justifications and satisfactions. And I most certainly do not hold that the development of the intellect is the only, or even the main, long-term educational goal. Whitehead begins his book 'The Aims of Education' with the famous sentence: 'Culture is activity of thought and receptiveness to beauty and humane feeling.' Even this first sentence does not say everything but it is a nutshell packed unusually tight. I believe that all of these are, indeed, attributes of the well-educated mind. However, I do not take Whitehead's order of mention as the true order of importance. We need not assume that he intended it so himself.

It may seem strange, then, that I have been placing so much emphasis on the intellectual, disembedded modes of thought. The explanation lies in the following argument.

Our kind of society needs these modes of thought, if for no other reason than that they underpin all our science and all our technology, giving us great practical power. It is power that we often abuse. For instance, it enables us to make bombs. Thus, though it serves good ends also, it is highly dangerous power for us to have; and yet I see no realistic prospect that we shall willingly give it up. We might, just possibly, learn to use it more wisely, with greater restraint and foresight. That is the best that can be hoped for.

If the argument is accepted so far, then the next step is to consider who is to have this power. In my view, it is of extreme social importance that it should be widely spread. I certainly do not mean that we should all, or most of us, become scientists. But we should not feel overwhelmed by science and technology – not daunted or shut out. We should know ourselves *capable* of the kind of thinking in which scientists and engineers professionally engage. Otherwise their activities are apt to seem as mysterious as those of the high priestly caste in a primitive tribe.

And likewise we (as many of us as possible – and certainly many more than at present) should feel ourselves capable of thinking like a philosopher, or like a specialist in any intellectual discipline – literature, politics, economics, education – at least to the extent of reading an introductory book on the subject and reflecting seriously on the arguments it contains.

I do not suppose that most people would want to read such books as a habitual activity, or even at all. I am talking about feeling confident that one could. It is the conviction of inability that is damaging. This is the deep damage – or part of the deep damage – that results from what we call 'educational failure'.

Widespread literacy at this level is evidently remote. But I am sure that we could move closer to it – and equally that we could find ourselves moving much further away. In this connection, any set of beliefs or values is damaging that leads teachers to neglect the *study* of language.

On the other hand, it is a grave error to suppose that what happens in school is the only thing affecting the outcome. This is a tempting mistake for those outside the schools – for society at large – to make. It offers society an easy way out of responsibility, making it possible to blame failure if not on lazy or stupid children then on misguided or incompetent teachers. But the truth is that children will not study language – or anything else – effectively if, for example, they are short of sleep, or if they have come out without breakfast, or if they have been abused and frightened, or if they belong to a sub-group that is given little credit for intellectual potential. Those who try to teach such children are constantly reminded of this fact. The rest of us should constantly remind ourselves.

d Methods and the individual child

I want now to guard against another misunderstanding, among the many that are always possible. When I argue for active, systematic teaching in the furtherance of literacy I am not arguing for regimented uniformity. Whatever we do, we should respect the individuality of the children we teach. Even if a way of teaching is good for the many, some may fail to thrive on it. When this becomes apparent, other ways should always be tried.

But notice that this is true no matter what method is being used. For instance, while most children enjoy stories rich in fantasy, some want fact because it interests them more. And some find fantasy terrifying. A famous example in this last category is the philosopher, Jeremy Bentham, who, by his own account, was an anxious child with an overly vivid imagination. Ghost stories, he tells us, were among the torments of his life. But even the story of Robinson Crusoe disturbed him, for he was not sure at first whether the Goat of the Cave might not be the devil. And fear of the devil made him quite unable to read 'The Pilgrim's Progress' (11).

Bentham's fears were extreme and seem to have been deliberately fed by the servants in his father's household. The fact that a few children are particularly vulnerable in this way does not mean that, as a general rule, we should offer only a bland story diet guaranteed never to provoke a shiver along the spine. I have a personal memory of reading John Bunyan's 'The Holy War' at a fairly early age and of being intrigued rather than frightened by the story of how Diabolus and 'that mighty giant Beelzebub' laid siege to the city of Mansoul. I think the book was made specially memorable for me by two things. First, it was a beautiful old edition with illustrations that caught my imagination. And secondly, as I read it I had my first dawning awareness of the nature of allegory: I came to suspect that Mansoul was not just a name on a par with Manchester. This was an insight that made a deep impression and opened up before me a whole new range of possibilities. But another child might have found it quite unexciting.

Who is to say in advance what will make a reading experience memorable for a given human being? For I also remember the delight I felt when I first managed to read, by myself, the name of a local cinema in a newspaper advertisement. I would be hard put to it to rank these two very different reading experiences in any order of significance in my mental life.

We cannot legislate for such flashes of delight; but we can work systematically to provide conditions that favour them. However no teaching programme, even if well-founded, should be followed slavishly. This is a principle of the utmost importance. A good teacher is always on the look-out for children with special attitudes and sensitivities and tries to respect these, as far as material and emotional resources allow.

*   *   *   *   *   *

6   Conclusion

Certain conclusions as to the development of the impersonal modes of thought seem inescapable: first that, if things are to improve, the foundations of intellectual competence should be laid early; second, that becoming literate in Olson's sense is one of these foundations; and third, that almost all children will become literate more easily and fully if they are given systematic help which is based on a good understanding of the nature of the enterprise but which never fails to respect them as individual learners.

However, this is not all that matters. Literacy learning has – should have – many strands. The 'bridging' experiences that I discussed earlier are of varying kinds, fulfilling different functions. Shared reading serves to capture the imagination, attune the ear and develop the sense of story. Embedded print fosters and clarifies important concepts about the communicative functions of written language. Materials which allow children to compose their first phrases and sentences without the need for pencil and paper open up a means of effective communication in written form. They focus attention on the role of individual words and bound morphemes, and on many basic features of sentence structure such as word order. They provide opportunities too for beginning to talk about language.

Then there is certainly a most important place for the reading of text which is very simple, but which is not stilted in its sentence forms and is linked to familiar and interesting themes. Its use gives a progressive sense of mastery over the new medium. It provides models for children's own written sentence production. It helps to lay the foundations of one of the main components of skilled reading, which is rapid and effortless word recognition. And it allows for an early introduction to easy non-fiction prose.

This blend of varied experience can continue right through the primary school, as shared reading gives way to independent reading of both fiction and non-fiction, and writing skills develop. While these processes go on, the children can also be encouraged to think about language, oral and written, and to extend their awareness of its structure. They can begin the systematic study of the language of books, a study valuable in itself and crucial for the maturing of literacy in the fullest sense.

'Nothing too much' is the best guiding principle (though notice that this does not imply 'anything goes'). The different strands should combine in different ways at different times. Boundless enthusiasm for any one of them is unwise. The general conclusion has to be that the receiving of systematic help with literacy learning – involving the use of good reading or language programmes – does not preclude and should not obstruct the experience of reading good books of all kinds for the joy of it. These complement one another. In educational debate, for some curious reason which I do not fully understand, we are constantly being led to suppose that we must choose either *a* or *b* when we urgently need both – and can perfectly well have both.

There is, most fortunately, no incompatibility between developing a love of literature, with all the personal enrichment which that brings, and developing the ways of handling language that favour clear, sustained rational thought. These can – and should – develop side by side, through the school years.

Notes

1   A recent paper by Hynds (1988) provides an example – a rather extreme one – of how the inadequacy of earlier theorising is being used now to try to discredit all reading schemes. Hynds says: 'Thinking of the rats, well-intentioned educators ... devised reading schemes'. The rats that he has in mind are those used in behavioural learning studies. He then goes on to give the impression that all reading schemes are based on behavioural concepts of the nature of learning.

This is just not true. It is not true now, and it was not true even when the influence of behaviourism was at its height. For instance, one reading scheme was written back in the 1950's by I A Richards, the distinguished literary critic and poet, and he was deeply opposed to behaviourism in any form. Unfortunately this scheme did not turn out to be one of Richards' most successful enterprises. Its guiding principles were logical rather than psychological.

I do not suppose that Hynds is guilty of deliberate distortion. I believe rather that his paper provides an example of the way passionate commitment can restrict what the mind admits as knowledge. It is a very general human problem. Think of the Holy Office and Galileo.

2   Research has established that most parents do speak to children in somewhat special ways, sometimes called 'motherese'. What is much less clear is the extent to which children are helped by various kinds of 'motherese' at various stages of development. The issues are highly complex and the evidence that would resolve them is not easy to obtain. (See Gleitman *et al,* 1984.)

3   Goodman was certainly not alone. The times in which he wrote were heady ones for developmental psychologists and for educators influenced by them. What should have been more often recalled as a corrective was Vygotsky's work dating from the early 1930's (though not published in English until 1962). Vygotsky was in no doubt about the distinction between speech and writing (or what he called 'oral speech' and 'written speech'). As he put it: 'Written speech is a separate linguistic function differing from oral speech in both structure and mode of functioning' (Vygotsky, 1962).

4   It is worth remarking at this point how much emphasis is given to reflection on wording by the writers of the recent Kingman Report (DES 1988). The Report talks of '. . . examining words and how each contributes to the meaning of a sentence' (p 9). It argues over and over again for the raising and extending of children's awareness of how language is structured and how it functions (ch 2, passim). There is no doubt that the writers believe that children should learn to attend closely to what is on the page.

5   'Normal' is itself ambiguous. It can mean 'average' with no value judgment implied; or it can carry an implication of desirability, as is evident when one thinks of the connotations of 'abnormal'. Smith also uses the word 'need', not in the exact sentence that I have used for illustration but in the same kind of way, for example as follows:

> '. . . we need be no more *aware* (his italics) of the words than we are of the paper (ie the paper they are printed on) if we are concerned with meaning.'

6   Young children do sometimes seem to 'play' with words, as in pre-sleep monologues, but it is hard to be sure of the significance of this. What I have said about the role of context relates to the use of speech in interpersonal communication.

7   Earlier examples do occur. Dunn (1987) provides one from the speech of a child just 21 months old. At breakfast there had been a distressing battle over food. Later in the day the child started a conversation with his mother by referring to this event:

> Child: Eat my Weetabix. Eat my Weetabix. Crying.
>
> Mother: Crying, weren't you? We had quite a battle. 'One more mouthful, Michael.' And what did you do? You spat it out!
>
> Child: ('cries').

I believe it to be significant that this early backward reference expressed strong remembered feeling. Notice that it did not depend on an ability to use the past tense.

8   Söderbergh (op cit) makes the same point:

> 'When it comes to *syntax* the differences between spoken and written language may be considerable, and a syntax that is too much deviant from that which the child uses in his spoken language may make the text impossible to read for him' (sic).

9   Some people, however, were in advance of their time in this respect, as is usually the case in the history of ideas. See, most notably, Huey (1908).

10   In fairness I must point out that Meek does not use this judgment to support the same conclusions as my own.

11   For an account of Bentham's fears and the effect of them on his later thinking see Ogden (1932).

REFERENCES

Cazden, C. Play with language and metalinguistic awareness: one dimension of language awareness. The Urban Review, 1974, 7, 1249-61.

Clay, M M. Reading errors and self-correction behaviour. British Journal of Educational Psychology, 1969, 39, 47-56.

Department of Education and Science. Report of the committee of inquiry into the teaching of English Language. HMSO 1988.

Doman, G. How to Teach your Baby to Read. New York: Random House 1964.

Donaldson, M. Children's Minds. London: Fontana, 1978.

Dunn, J. Understanding feelings: the early stages. In Bruner, J and Haste, H (Eds): Making Sense: The Child's Construction of the World. London and New York: Methuen, 1987.

Gleitman, L R, Newport, E L and Gleitman, H. The current status of the motherese hypothesis. Journal of Child Language, 1984, 11, 43-79.

Goodman, K S. Reading: the key is in children's language. The Reading Teacher, 1972 (March), 505-508.

Heath, S B. The functions and uses of literacy. In de Castell, S, Luke, A and Egan, K (Eds): Literacy, Society and Schooling. Cambridge: Cambridge University Press, 1986.

Hynds, J. In pursuit of a little understanding. Books for Keeps, 52, 1988.

Huey, E B. The Psychology and Pedagogy of Reading. Cambridge, Mass: MIT Press, 1968. (First published 1908).

McNeill, D. Psycholinguistics: A New Approach. New York: Harper and Row, 1987.

McAleavy, T. Conflict in Ireland. History 13-16 Project. Edinburgh: Holmes McDougall, 1987. (Published under the aegis of the School Curriculum Development Committee, London.)

Meek, M. Learning to Read. London: The Bodley Head, 1982.

Midgeley, M. Evolution as a Religion. London and New York: Methuen, 1985.

Ogden, C K. Bentham's Theory of Fictions. London: Kegan Paul, Trench, Trubner & Co Ltd, 1932.

Olson, D. 'See! Jumping!' Some oral language antecedents of literacy. In Goelman, H, Oberg, A and Smith, F (Eds). Awakening to Literacy. London: Heinemann Educational Books, 1984.

Reid, J F. An investigation of thirteen beginners in reading. Acta Psychologica, 1958, 14, 295-313.

Reid, J F. Sentence structure in reading primers. Research in Education, 1970, 3, 23-37.

Reid, J F. Breakthrough in Action: An Independent Evaluation of 'Breakthrough to Literacy'. London: Longman for the Schools Council, 1974.

Reid, J F. Into print: reading and language growth. *In* Donaldson, M, Grieve, R and Pratt, C (Eds): Early Childhood Development and Education. New York and London: The Guilford Press, 1983.

Scottish Certificate of Education, Standard Grade. Revised Arrangements in English. Scottish Examination Board, 1987.

Smith, F. Reading. Cambridge: Cambridge University Press, 1978.

Söderbergh, R. Early reading as language acquisition. System, 1981, 9, 207-13.

Strickland, R. The language of elementary school children: its relation to the language of reading textbooks and the quality of reading of selected children. Bulletin of the School of Education, University of Indiana, 1962, Vol 38, No 2.

Tizard, B and Hughes, M. Young Children Learning. London: Fontana, 1984.

Vygotsky, L S. Thought and Language. Cambridge, Mass: MIT Press, 1962.

Weber, R M. A linguistic analysis of first-grade reading errors. Reading Research Quarterly, 1970, 5, 427-51.

Whitehead, A N. The Aims of Education. London: Williams and Norgate, 1932.

LINKED

This book is to be returned on or before
the last date stamped below.